CONRAN OCTOPUS CONTEMPORARY

water features

CONRAN OCTOPUS CONTEMPORARY
water features

David Stevens

conran
OCTOPUS

contents

introduction	8	fish & wildlife	86
planning & design	10	address book	92
materials & methods	54	index	94
planting	78	acknowledgments	96

introduction

The power of water in your garden

Water is both simple and complex, a giver of life, the key to growth and the largest single surface on our planet. It shapes continents and drives weather systems. It has been harnessed, channelled and used for our service and our pleasure. Water is inexorably woven into the history of gardens. It appears everywhere, from the gardens of ancient Egypt and Mesopotamia to the most avant-garde compositions of today.

Water brings movement, sound, reflections and peace. It offers a habitat for plants, fish and wildlife but, perhaps above all else, it allows us to control and enjoy the most primeval of elements. Like gardens themselves, water offers endless opportunities. The only limits are those of our own imagination. As with gardens, it is all too easy to fall into the trap of over complication when designing with water. In both cases, the result is a visual disaster.

In this book I have set out to demystify the use of water in the garden and to show how it can be blended into the whole design. Being a designer, I understand the importance of looking at the garden, house and surrounding

environment in the 'round'. I am aware of the necessity to create a composition that suits you and your family, and I am conscious that the best gardens are essentially simple, always serving you and never the dogma of fashion.

Whether you have a fondness for formality and control, for tumbling streams, drilled millstones or polished granite spheres floating on low-pressure water jets, this book will guide you through making a choice and installing your chosen feature.

It has never been easier to use water. The old, complicated methods of constructing features from concrete and other cumbersome materials have largely been superseded, and with them, much of the expense and maintenance traditionally associated with water features. So there really is no excuse to do without water – the most exciting element in garden design.

Left *By crossing or dividing water you will find yourself manipulating its very nature.*
Above *These simple, horizontal pipes contrast with the vertical lines of the planting to great effect.*
Opposite *Moving water has a life of its own. Its ever-changing patterns dance and swirl in the sunlight.*

planning

& design

Many of us would love to have water in the garden, but there is no point in rushing into things. Digging a haphazard hole or buying an off-the-peg pool will get you nowhere if you haven't thought carefully about what you want, where you want it, and how it will blend into the overall design of the garden.

first steps

Water is a natural element and an essential part of the landscape. To tame or copy it, bringing it within the confines of the garden, takes sensitivity and skill. Water gardening is a growth industry and ever more specialist centres are opening, many of which have a huge range of products and equipment. The danger is impulse buying as this can result in a feature that is totally at odds with your garden. More often than not, it will be a pseudo-natural watercourse with plastic cascades that drop into a poorly constructed pool surrounded by crazy paving. While I am far from a gardening snob, I honestly feel that such an approach demeans the potential of water and your enjoyment of it.

In most situations one must choose between a natural effect or an artificial feature that is positively sculptural or architectural. Both approaches are entirely valid and both rely for their success on blending in with the surrounding composition rather than fighting against it. This means that the water feature should be considered at the design stage of the garden, and not simply tacked on as an afterthought.

Inspiration can come from many places including books, garden shows, television programmes or magazines. If you take time in planning your garden then you can gather visual images together to create a 'moodboard'. This will help you to rationalize your ideas. In all probability, your garden will be either formal or informal and the features within the composition will follow suit, which is where you need to start making some positive decisions.

In many ways formal features are relatively easy to plan, as they link decisively with the geometry that surrounds them. Informal features require additional skills as they must look as though they are natural. In my experience, it is almost impossible to achieve this end by looking at pictures, the simple reason being that you have to 'feel' water in order to understand its character. The best thing to do is to get out into the country to see how nature does it. Upland areas have enormous character. Take a camera and see how the rock is laid down in strata, how valley spurs interlock with one another with a stream running through the bottom and how water cascades over it all. Take photographs of falls, see how the rock is undercut, how the stream splits, tumbles and re-forms. Look at pools, rills, boulders and slides, and see how trees and plants grow in naturally formed crevices. In other words, get into it all. The environment you are trying to create should not be just a currant bun stuck in the middle of a garden, with assorted lumps of concrete and sad, sparse shrubs. Water is exciting and dynamic, so make the most of it and enjoy!

Having said all that, the more complex water features are, the more expense is involved. It is easy to underestimate the cost of creating a garden and in basic terms it will be the 'hard landscape' that will take the lion's share of any budget. This will include paving, walling and any major construction work, of which water will be a part. Rock, terracing, pumps and other equipment are not cheap, but if well chosen and correctly constructed they should last a lifetime. Pumps have improved enormously over the past few years and rarely fail. In addition, they cost virtually nothing to run, so although the initial investment may seem steep, it is a worthwhile one. Of course, one of the advantages of preparing a design for the whole garden is that you can carry out the work in stages, as and when energy, time and funds allow. In other words, as long as space is allocated for a water feature it could easily be phased in as part of a longer-term development programme.

The siting of water is vitally important and should be included in the initial planning process. An open area, away from overhanging trees, would be ideal. Ultimate success, however, depends not just on the positioning of a feature, but on a variety of factors, including aquatic planting, adequate oxygenation and the attraction of wildlife to the feature, all of which will be discussed later in the book.

Water is endlessly fascinating. There is a place for it in any garden, but the real secret is how to integrate it

Above left *For centuries Japanese gardens have influenced Western design. Water often plays a central role, appearing in pools or flumes and flowing over carefully positioned rocks.*
Left *Even the smallest yard has room for water in some form. Here it is blended into the overall composition with cascades of planting.*
Opposite *Understatement is everything in terms of design and this pot floats on a perfect mirror of water, the low hedge containing the vision.*

successfully. If your garden is on a slope this is an obvious advantage. Changes in level can be handled either formally or informally, with water dropping down from one level to another. Perhaps you have a fine view with an open area in front of it. A site like this offers wonderful potential for a calm, reflective pool. The water could reflect both the view and the moods of an ever-changing sky. A simple, but no less effective, option is offered by the wall of a tiny yard, where spouts, masks or bowls can transform an otherwise dull situation into a sonorous and entertaining area.

Above *There is always tension between static planting and the movement of water. In this instance the tension has been heightened by the subtle artifice of the frog. Humour is another factor that can draw the eye and provide a focal point.*
Opposite *A contemporary water feature links naturally with a modern building and here the pools step down to the lowest curving shape, a form that takes its line from the house itself.*

Above *A contrast in style, if handled boldly, can be both surprising and dramatic.*
The crisp white walls of the house set up a wonderful dialogue with the free-form pool and dark rocks.
A single tree adds vertical emphasis while the dark water provides a visual link with the rocks.

Below *If you are going to control water then do it properly and don't take prisoners. The precision of this feature is sheer poetry, the dark, crisp paving framing the rill and defining the steps.*

Above *Contemporary gardens should be just that, with positive lines and a real sense of purpose. The flowing curve of this raised pool makes a positive link with the building. The use of common materials makes a bond between deck and pool and there is also a physical connection with the river view.*

choosing a style

Every garden should have a general theme or style and the water feature should be part of its design. The style of your garden depends on you. If water is to be part of the garden it must blend in with the overall composition. For example, it would be wrong to slap an informal pool down in the middle of a crisp, formal terrace.

In most gardens the house provides the starting point for a design, often suggesting a style. For example, a traditional building with a regular façade may well have a formal garden to match. There is also a natural progression of space. The design should become less architectural as you move away from the house. Any garden elements, including water, should follow this progression. Rectangular, interlocking pools near the building could give way to free-form streams, cascades and ponds at the furthest point from the house.

No style should be a straitjacket. At the end of the day, you must consider your needs and decide what makes you feel comfortable. Remember, fashion has wasted more good money than anything else.

Right *Style is a creative blend of personality and architectural connections. There is enormous tension here between the tiled rectangles that barely touch one another and the echoing shapes of the hedge. Water provides a linking element, tying the composition together and adding subtle reflections.*

formal

Formality suggests a regular pattern, a feeling of control, geometry and tradition. In fact, formal gardens can also be quite the opposite, ultra-modern and built with high-tech materials. Whatever their period, they rely on a balanced composition that is mirrored from side to side or from end to end.

Water is delightful in a formal design. It can be organized into pools set within or around a terrace, flanking a path or a main axis or acting as a division between different parts of the garden. It might be used as a rill, linking a series of pools, a water staircase or simply a dramatic full stop at the end of a vista.

Above Formal designs often look their best under minimalist conditions. The rhythmical blocks of low hedge are tied together by long pools, while the reflective balls act as punctuation marks.
Right The permanence of statuary and the transience of a fountain set up a fascinating dialogue. A background hedge marks the boundary of this particular garden room.
Opposite A balance between youth and age produces an unusual contrast, reinforced by the centrally placed bowl and pool. The background wall provides the canvas for a three-dimensional composition.

asymmetric

Asymmetry was born out of the Modern Movement. It was a reaction against formality, which was seen as a rigid and dated style. Asymmetric designs still rely on geometry, but instead of the pattern being mirrored, balance is achieved by shapes or features of different visual weights coming into equilibrium by careful positioning within the overall design. For example, a terrace might be built up from a series of overlapping rectangles made up of paving, planting and water. All of these would reflect an underlying grid that picks up on the geometry of the adjoining building. Water could be set at ground level or raised, with an upper pool cascading onto the lower level.

Above Hard and soft elements are positioned in perfect harmony; the crisp reflections of the water providing the ideal link between the two.
Left Taking a zigzag through a garden, in this case over water, increases the feeling of space. The slatted stepping decks are at right angles to one another, echoing the background screen.
Below Decks always harmonize well with water, both being natural elements. There is an additional visual link here between the angled pools and the timberwork.

In the wider setting, a substantial water feature could be positioned some way down the garden. It might work to offset a garden building, arbour or group of trees elsewhere. While asymmetry still requires control and sensitivity, it is often an excellent style adjoining modern houses, or those with an irregular outline.

Opposite There is great power in the cobble divide between the upper and lower pools. The raised water is also irresistibly tactile, being within such easy dabbling height.

informal

In many ways this is the most difficult style of all and it is certainly the most abused. It relies for its success on an ability to understand the workings and shapes of nature, whether in the form of a gently meandering river or the rough and tumble of an upland stream. The over-used kidney-shaped pool is rarely found in the natural environment, nor are pools formed from the outline of a hose pipe cast on the ground and kicked aimlessly into some convoluted pattern.

Sensitivity is all in an informal situation. You might have virtually the whole of a garden given over to a naturalistic pool lushly planted with indigenous species, perhaps adding a beautifully detailed deck to give a dash of control. Alternatively, your garden may move from the architectural to the informal in a smooth transition of space. Both approaches are quite valid.

Right *An informal style created with flowing lines, soft planting, smooth, bubbling boulders or cascading waterfalls. The secret is to reproduce an unconscious simulation of the landscape, using natural materials and subtle effects. This fall is perfectly constructed, the rocks are all laid to a definite bedding plane. The sound of running water will be particularly beautiful on a summer day.*

Opposite left *A well-worn piece of timber acts as a channel for a small waterfall that drops into a rocky pool, demonstrating that found materials can be just as effective as shop-bought ones.*

Opposite right *A large boulder, drilled through its centre, makes an effective centrepiece. The rock needs to be securely supported underneath the water.*

Opposite below *The crisp lines of a white wall strike a note of formality in an otherwise informal composition. The horizontal line of the wall is cleverly set off by vertical planting.*

ways with water

Although the variety of ways in which water can be used are limitless, we have already seen that any feature should be tailored to suit the overall garden style. Water is a rich habitat and your feature could support a whole range of plants, fish and other wildlife. Most ponds and pools are suitable for fish, and a larger pool can also be a haven for wildfowl. Fish can live in streams and rills, but these features are more likely to suit planting. In a pool the planting could be lush and informal, while in a rill it might be unashamedly architectural.

Bog gardens are a plantsman's paradise. No irrigation is needed here and the plants produce dynamic foliage that lasts all summer long. On a smaller scale, my own cobble and boulder feature at home is fascinating and it is also safe for young children. Or why not go really high-tech and build a 'water-port' like the one opposite? Remember that the ideas that follow are intended to act as a catalyst: the only limit to what you can achieve with water is your imagination.

Right The effects that you can achieve with water are endless, they can be subtle, straightforward or downright humorous. The secret of success lies not just in imagination but also in the construction. The feature must function perfectly, but the mechanics of it must remain invisible. The end result may be bold or, as here, deliciously delicate, the humour shining through.

Above *In my own gardens I test the dynamics of water to their limits, playing endlessly with colour, movement, planting and anything else that will take the art form forward. This spectacular water slide is divided into alternate chutes of water and plants. It runs out from the house, over a combined sitting and drive area, across a pool and into the bed on the far side. The construction of all this had to be worked out from scratch, the pumps and pipework concealed and the whole thing made watertight to protect the people sitting beneath. It worked beautifully.*

pools & ponds

As we have seen, the style of your water feature can vary from the strictly formal to the completely naturalistic, and pools and ponds are no exception. Whichever style you choose, what first comes to mind when thinking of pools and ponds is a large and relatively open area of water. In purely practical terms, the larger the pool, the easier it will be to maintain. This is because its size will allow you to achieve the ideal balance of plants, fish and other aquatic life. Pests, such as mosquitoes, will be controlled by the 'friendly' inmates of your pool. It is difficult to achieve this healthy balance in pools less than 2m (6½ft) square, so try to make them at least as big as this, and larger if you possibly can.

If we think of the garden as a natural extension of the house, it makes sense to start by planning the pools around the building. The link between inside and out is a strong one and, in extreme circumstances, water can actually be planned to extend from an interior room to an outside one, separated only by a sheet of glass dipping just below the surface. Fish and plants can live in either environment. In the case of a swimming pool, which can be equally decorative, people can even swim from house to garden!

The dimensions of any pool close to the house should normally reflect the underlying paving module, fitting comfortably into the pattern rather than breaking across it. In other words, if you lifted out a number of slabs, an area of deck or some sections of an overall design grid that is based on the proportions of the house, the pool would fit neatly into it.

***Right** Ponds and pools can be as large or small as you like. This is a perfect study in the art of the miniature, and it brings great intimacy to this corner of the garden. The pattern on the bowl is a subtle touch as is echoes the form of the lily.*

***Opposite** By paying attention to detail and using vernacular materials you are bound to create a worthwhile composition. Although this is essentially a formal design, the cobbles soften the outline, blending it into the path in the foreground. The slight change in level makes the rill drip into the lower pool, providing both sound and movement.*

Right *The character of a pool can be greatly influenced by plants. In this pool plants are the defining element, practically covering the whole surface. Such an approach both softens the surrounding paving and blends the feature into the wider garden.*

If we think of the garden as a natural extension of the house, it makes sense to start by planning the pools around the building

The simplest pool will be set just below the terrace surface with the surrounding paving acting as a precise coping. Rather more complex designs can incorporate split-level pools. The higher level might be set at 450mm (18in) so that it can double as an occasional seat. The water would flow over a sill into the lower pool. In this case, the lower pool should be considerably larger than the upper one, otherwise it will overflow when the circulating pump is switched off. Such a composition could also include split-level planting, built-in seating or even a barbecue.

Moving further away from the house, the shapes can become progressively less formal, echoing those of the surrounding design. The pool might have a paved surround or be a more naturalistic type of pond, bounded by grass, planting or with a full-blown bog garden around it. There could be a deck, sitting area or summerhouse, but whatever the composition a pool sited at some distance from the house and its surrounds will become a major focal point.

Remember that the view to or from such a feature really is an important consideration – there's no point in gazing fondly at the back of your garage or its reflection in the water (unless it is incredibly attractive!) – so make sure that you think about this when deciding where to position your pool.

Left *Reflections play endlessly with light. They can dance with a breeze or mirror the view on a still day. The essence of this design is subtle movement, from the stone bubble fountain in the foreground, through the rill with its strong directional emphasis, to the calm sheet of water framed by paving and a low hedge. The overall feeling is one of control, and this sits comfortably with the regular façade of the house.*

streams, rills & canals

All of these features suggest both visual and physical movement. They lead the eye in a given direction, and form a physical link between separate areas of water. Again, we have a division between the formal geometry of rills and canals and the informality of streams.

Historic houses and gardens are often richly formal. There are wonderful lessons to be learnt by visiting them, armed with a camera and notebook. Sir Edwin Lutyens, the great English architect and garden designer, was a master of geometry. He used superbly detailed rills, pools and canals to create subtle links between the house and garden. Of the two, rills are narrow, often only 300mm (12in) or so across, and this visually compresses the water to create a real feeling of tension as the feature runs from one larger area of water to another. For a rill to be really effective it needs to be as long as reasonably possible. In a large garden this might be several hundred metres.

Rills normally contain little planting as the space is so limited. However, smaller reeds and rushes can provide delicate verticals against a long horizontal line. Canals are also long and comparatively narrow, but on a far larger scale. They firmly belong to the formal school, whether this be traditional or modern. When positioned with sensitivity they have an enormous potential to draw the eye and to provide stunning reflections. In my opinion they are best planted with low-growing aquatics, such as lilies. Fountains detract from their ability to mirror the sky or neighbouring features.

Right *The success of rills and canals relies on the control of an essentially powerful element, while retaining its inherent mystery: here a formal structure combined with the dark surface achieves this balance.*
Opposite *Water is astonishing in its power, seeming to slash its way through the surrounding paving.*

The real secret of success is to create something that looks natural

Below *Streams are alive with movement and in a garden this can take many different forms. This white cobble beach would rarely be found in nature, but in a controlled setting it brings reflected light and a sharp contrast to the immediate surroundings.*

Above *The juxtaposition of architectural and natural features sets up a fascinating dialogue, the one enhancing the other with the strong lines of the foreground providing a focus for the rocks.*

Streams are full of movement and they need a slope, natural or artificial, to work well. Once again, scale is everything and as a general rule the more generous the feature the better. A stream's character can be upland or lowland, the former with rock and flying water, the latter much calmer, with reduced flow rates and lusher planting. The gradient of your garden will tell you which is the most appropriate choice. Great care should be taken in creating artificial slopes to make them look convincing. The real secret of success is to create something that looks natural. This is another motive for getting to know the environment. Streams ebb and flow, they have pools that are deep, rapids that are shallow, they are undercut on the outside of bends and they deposit silt on the inside. If you are a kid at heart, and I am, there is nothing better than messing about on the river, or stream, so go for it!

Above *Water can so easily tease you from one garden room to the next, the stream giving way to a rill, which in turn feeds the pool. Pyramids of foliage guard the space, providing a frame of vertical lines above the reflective floor.*

fountains

Fountains are the exclamation marks of a garden, demanding as much, if not more, attention than any other major focal point. They can range from the simplest jet that just breaks the surface with a bubble, to grand affairs that soar many metres into the air.

The simplest fountain is a single plume. In addition to its visual value, it can help to aerate a pool, benefiting fish during hot weather. The height or volume of the jet will relate to the size of the pool. If a tall plume is installed in a small pond the slightest breeze will quickly empty the feature. The sight and sound of water on a summer day is irresistible. A small bubble jet is the perfect addition to an intimate sitting area.

On a practical level, the most common method of driving a fountain is the submersible pump. Many have adjustable valves to raise or lower the flow. If installed correctly they are perfectly safe and run for many years at minimal expense. In between these two extremes are all kinds of variations, some of which can be astonishingly beautiful, but some of which, unfortunately, can be mere ill-conceived gimmicks. As with most other elements in the garden, it is generally the simple schemes that look the best.

If you happen to have a lake then you may want to be more expansive, perhaps positioning a monster at its

Left *Fountains are the dancers in the world of water. Classical or contemporary, they add vibrancy and movement, linking the second and third dimensions together. There is great rhythm here, not just in the relationship of these Perspex tubes but in the bubbles that rise and swirl through them.*
Opposite *Any radius needs a pivot. In this case it is provided by a simple plume rising from the circular, cobble-filled pool. The curving background wall holds the design together; it is a perfect backdrop for the cascade of foliage that works in opposition to the fountain.*

centre. To my mind this is simply showing off and, quite apart from the expense, smacks of ostentation. I'd rather have the reflections, which are destroyed by any kind of fountain or induced movement.

You have only to visit some of the great Renaissance gardens in Italy to see that there are no limits to the possibilities of water. Equally stunning features are being created for gardens today on a smaller and more domestic scale. A great friend of mine designs 'flat' fountains made from sheets of stainless steel of various sizes. Slots are cut in the sheets so that water spills in ripples and rills over the polished surface. The effect is magical.

Kugels are one of my favourite forms of fountain. They are made from perfectly formed stone spheres which can measure up to 2m (6½ft) across. The sphere is set in a matching stone cup, where it 'floats' on low-pressure jets of water, turning slowly this way and that, catching the sun and the imagination in a continuous pattern of reflective movement.

Left *There is something wonderfully mysterious about water welling up and over this dark bowl, the whole arrangement set about with flower and foliage.*
Above *Pyramids have a unique, primeval and visual force that dates back to the Egyptians. Water associates perfectly with them, the stepped sides echoing a chiselled rock face. Rills add control in this situation, tying the feature into the wider garden.*

Above *This is a wonderful example of an organic water feature. It echoes the shape of tropical urchin shells. Groups of three always look comfortable and the whole arrangement is perfectly set off by the pale gravel that covers the sump and mechanics beneath. Low planting and grasses are the perfect foil, the tufted shapes enhancing rather than fighting against the rounded domes.*

wall-mounted features

Many gardens are too small for a pool but this need not prevent you from bringing water into your design. In town gardens the wall area is often considerably greater than that of the floor, but it is frequently ignored or under-used. Once we start to consider the potential of the vertical planes of the garden we start to realize that walls can support all kinds of planting in baskets or boxes, built-in furniture or, of course, water.

By now it will be clear that the choice of feature should be defined by the period of the building and the style of the garden. The problem is that most garden centres stock a preponderance of so-called 'classical' items – cherubs relieving themselves or lions endlessly regurgitating water that have inevitably devalued the currency of classical garden water features. Don't buy the first thing you see, shop around and think of the style you wish to enhance. While there is nothing wrong with a classical item in a formal garden, there are an increasing number of designers offering abstract or just good contemporary, wall-mounted features. The best places to hunt these out are garden shows, where you will find an enormous range of innovative work.

Water has a powerful visual attraction – it draws the eye. Remember this when choosing a position for your water feature. All too often a mask or bowl is placed

Remember those vital design ingredients of tension, mystery and surprise

Right With a wall-mounted feature the spout, or spouts, is as much an attraction as the water itself. These can be classical or contemporary – here there is a real contrast between the mythical fish and the dry stone wall behind. This is an important point as the background should always be low key, allowing the feature to shine through.

Right *In an intimate space you can raise a feature close to eye level. Water can change direction and these copper stems and cups seem to mimic arum lilies, themselves lovers of water. Copper is not only easy to work but over time it acquires a wonderful patina.*

directly opposite a door or window. By drawing the eye, it has the effect of foreshortening the space. In terms of overall design, it may be better to think of a position just out of immediate view. The enticing sound of the water positioned out of sight, but just within earshot, will draw you down to another part of the garden, increasing the feeling of space. Remember those vital design ingredients of tension, mystery and surprise. These elements allow a garden to unfold in a series of different moods and 'rooms'.

If you are creative and competent, why not design and install your own water feature? It could be a series of polished copper cups set vertically with one overflowing into another, finishing in a bowl at the lowest level. One or more upright Perspex tubes of different heights could have water welling up and over them, economical on space and wonderful when lit from below at night. Alternatively, on a classical theme, you might find a stone mask and use it as the base for a striking feature. This would be easy enough to drill to accept a pipe and spout. Designing your own feature enables you to input part of your own personality into your garden and create something that is completely in tune with its mood.

The construction of all of these features, which I shall look at in greater detail later on, is quite straight-forward, using a small sump, submersible pump and simple pipe-work. They are also low maintenance – all that is needed is for the water to be topped up to compensate for evaporation.

Above *While the classical pouting and spouting mask is ever popular, it can be worked in a thousand different ways. Tufa rock suggests a grotto, water cascading into a damp green fernery below.*
Opposite *Taps, on the other hand, are water workhorses but can be transformed into a decorative element with a little imagination.*

The enticing sound of water positioned out of site, but just within earshot, will draw you down to another part of the garden, increasing the feeling of space

small-scale features

Of all water features, these can be the most innovative and they are certainly my own favourites. They not only fit into the smallest of areas but can also be made from a vast range of different materials.

The whole trend started off with the simple millstone fountain: enormous and durable, they create impressive features. A genuine millstone, which naturally has a hole in the middle, is positioned over a sump that usually takes the form of a water tank. A submersible pump is positioned at the bottom and connected to a pipe that

The whole trend started off with the simple millstone fountain: enormous and durable, they create impressive features

runs up through the stone, stopping just below the top surface. When the pump is switched on, water flows up and over the surface, then returns to the sump in a continuous cycle. The whole feature is often surrounded by loose cobbles or larger stones, together with planting. Today you can buy imitation millstones. While some of these almost look the part, many of them are decidedly false, being poorly constructed from fibreglass. The real point of a millstone is its size. Most real ones measure at least 1m (3ft 3in) across, while off-the-peg versions are a half or a third of that and look puny and feeble as a result.

Many years ago we started experimenting with a whole range of other materials, using the same principle of a sump, pump and connecting pipe to create all kinds of different effects. I remember that the first was an old slate pier head, some 600mm (2ft) square, with gently sloping sides. When a hole was drilled through the

Above *Isn't this just drop-dead gorgeous? I saw this copper leaf at a flower show some years ago and I have wanted it ever since! There is supreme subtlety and craftsmanship here, water being gently pumped up and over the surface. The secret is to blend it into a leafy background, so that you have to look twice to appreciate what is really going on.*

Right *This is a pure study in the relationship of different forms and textures, the glistening water boulder contrasting with the ribbed hosta leaves in the background. Ferns provide yet another foreground shape, revelling in the damp conditions.*

Opposite *When constructed properly and sited with sensitivity, this kind of feature is hard to beat in a confined space. Simplicity is often the key and the arrangement should flow gently rather than gush. When using bowls or containers, do check that they are frost proof as the combination of water and freezing conditions can be deadly.*

Above *You don't need a torrent to create a focal point, just a small change of level and imagination. The secret here is to adjust the flow and the angle of the slide so that water drops cleanly into the pool below. The warped timber slats offer a delightful feeling of informality, but they may need renewing on a regular basis if rot sets in.*

middle, water slid over the polished surface and looked wonderful. Exactly the same technique can be used for a fine glazed or terracotta bowl standing in a cobble bed. The feed pipe is sealed through the base of the bowl, which is filled with water. The pump is activated and water gushes, or wells, depending on how you valve the flow, over the edges and back into the sump. Try lying the bowl down; use two bowls, or three, of different diameters or heights – the permutations are endless.

Smooth or rough boulders can be drilled and used in the same way. I have just designed the most beautiful stainless-steel water boulder, a highly polished hemisphere set in a bed of ruby-red glass beads that sparkle in the sun. Perhaps the greatest advantage of all these features is their safety. Provided construction is carried out correctly and the sump is quite secure, there are no areas of open water that might be a danger to toddlers. I do of course exclude an open bowl from this category. Common sense must be applied when choosing the right feature.

structural features

This is where the big-time imagination comes into play – and why not! Most of us are far too conservative when it comes to introducing water into our gardens. There are any number of ways to employ it on a large scale and the effects are wonderful.

Everybody knows about car ports, but few people have a 'water port'. We built the one shown on page 29 from a sloping structure of steel and clear Perspex, angled down from the house towards a pool. Water is pumped to the top and slides down the Perspex, creating a spectacular combination of sound, reflection and movement. Water pergolas can be constructed in much the same way, with catchment pools to either side of the pergola, and a similar treatment could be used for a water arch. High-level planting can be incorporated into any of these structures, being housed within integral troughs that have irrigation built in.

Water walls are also spectacular and can be constructed from any number of materials. A trough along the top overflows and spills water down the wall into a long pond below. Finally, water stairs are yet another variation on the theme of falling water. They work with a submersible pump circulating water from bottom to top. The effect of the water gliding over and down the stairs is magical, particularly when lit by dancing beams of sunlight.

Right *'Structural' means just that – it implies a feeling of permanence and stability. Such features often provide dynamic focal points, leading the eye positively across or through the garden and terminating the view with a definite full stop. Here the raised rill beckons you towards the white picture-frame walls, where a canvas of water is punctuated by a fountain jet. There is great perspective here that is sharpened by the austerity of simple foliage set against the walls.*

Right *This is a contemporary Mediterranean garden that I built to reflect the harshness of the local landscape and subsequently brought alive with water. A major feature was the water curtain, made from rusting scaffold tube to reflect the colour of the surrounding landscape. Water drops gently but steadily along the length of the feature, setting up ripples that bring the pool alive with sound and movement.*

bog gardens

I've left the best to last. To have a bog garden is to have plants – and what plants! The real joy about such an area is the simple fact that you never have to water it and everything grows like mad. Of course, you have to choose the right species for the site, but many of these are really spectacular, from the huge leaves of *Gunnera manicata*, fantastic in a large garden but definitely not for the faint hearted, to the delicacy of astilbe or bog primulas which are more suitable for a smaller garden. There are hundreds of others and real favourites include hostas, ligularias, rodgersia, rheum and iris.

In visual and practical terms, a boggy area naturally adjoins a stream or pool, rarely being found as an isolated feature. It will need to be linked with the main area of water so that moisture can seep in. A bog garden is a damp area but it needs drainage or it will stagnate and be unable to support plant life.

Above *Foliage is the crowning glory of a bog garden and huge plants like* **Gunnera manicata** *can absorb all the moisture they need from the damp ground. The maintenance of such planting combinations is really restricted to thinning out when necessary.*

Right above and below *Foliage can be dramatic and so can flowers, particularly when they are used in great sweeps and drifts of colour as though someone had just cast bucketfuls of bloom over the garden. These bog primulas are particularly effective combined with species like* Lobelia cardinalis, *iris, astilibe and lythrum.*

materials

& methods

The best water features look either completely natural or crisply architectural and the secret of both is impeccable construction. While most techniques are straight forward, they need to be fully understood, which in turn asks for a degree of practicality and a knowledge of the materials involved. In this section I will take you through all of the techniques, letting you into a few trade secrets on the way.

using liners

Over the past 20 years pool liners have revolutionized construction of water features. The easy availability of durable, relatively low-cost liners which are quick and easy to install has made it possible for anyone with a basic level of skills and knowledge to build a simple water feature in their own garden. Additionally, liners are extremely adaptable, lending themselves to the construction of various styles of feature, from pools and waterfalls to streams and rills. Liners are sheets of plastic or, more durable still, tough butyl rubber which can be bought in different grades or thicknesses. All good garden centres and aquatic centres sell liners in

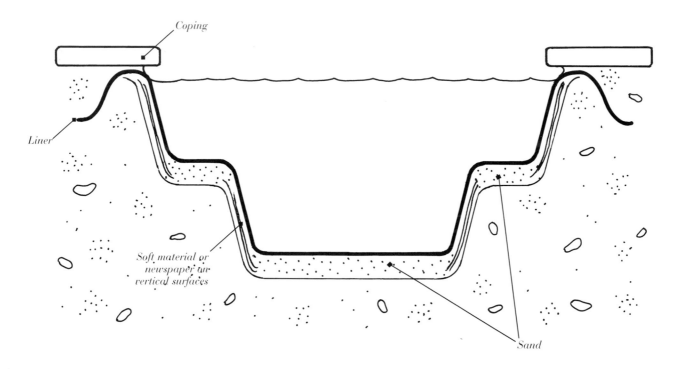

Coping

Liner

Soft material or newspaper on vertical surfaces

Sand

Above and opposite *Although flexible liners have become invaluable in pools and water features, they need to be concealed completely with coping if they are to be visually effective. They are tough, but care needs to be taken in construction. Sharp stones should be removed and the sheet should be bedded on a layer of sand. Smooth out the liner and run water into the pool to mould it to the excavation. Trim any excess liner away and lay paving, or another material, to overhang the edges.*

standard sizes. If you are building a pool to a non-standard size, you can follow this simple formula to estimate the size of the sheet that you need: add twice the depth to both the maximum length and width of the proposed pool or feature. If you are contemplating the construction of a water feature covering a very large area, you can get sections of liner welded together to your specifications. This technique can also be used for smaller, rectangular pools, where liners can be welded into a box shape so that they fit exactly into the area

Right and below *Beaches provide an attractive visual transition between water and dry land. They also conceal the liner and allow wildlife, such as frogs and small mammals, easy access to the water. The liner is bedded on 100mm (4in) of sand and covered with either soil, which allows aquatics to root easily, or mortar, which offers physical protection. Materials used to construct the beach should be compatible with the overall composition. Don't make the beach too regular as this will look artificial. Mix up the cobbles and other stone to create a more natural effect.*

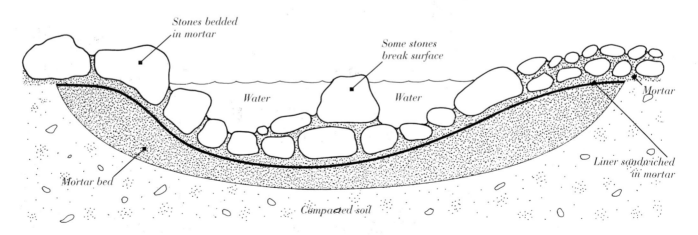

Stones bedded in mortar

Some stones break surface

Water

Water

Mortar

Mortar bed

Liner sandwiched in mortar

Compacted soil

Right and below *The secret to building an effective informal waterfall system is concealment of the liner, to make the feature look as natural as possible. The liner is laid over sand on horizontal surfaces and behind the vertical walls that separate the various levels. These walls should be built with solid concrete foundations as this will help to stabilize the whole feature. The principles of construction of informal waterfall systems are similar to those of formal systems – the difference lies in the materials chosen.*

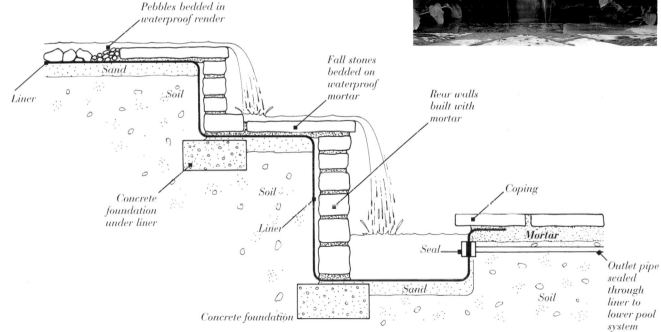

Pebbles bedded in
waterproof render

Sand

Liner

Soil

Fall stones
bedded on
waterproof
mortar

Concrete
foundation
under liner

Soil

Rear walls
built with
mortar

Liner

Coping

Mortar

Seal

Outlet pipe
sealed
through
liner to
lower pool
system

Concrete foundation

Sand

Soil

allocated for them, doing away with the need for complicated tucks and folds at the corners. Black liners are the best choice for most applications as they are virtually invisible when covered with water. Avoid patterned or coloured liners, particularly blue ones or those with simulated pebbles, as they look awful.

Concealment of the liner is an important consideration when designing a water feature. There is nothing worse than seeing a strip of wrinkled plastic or rubber lying around the top of a pool. Provided the pool rim is absolutely level and the surrounding coping overhangs the water by about 4cm (1½in), then the resulting shadow disguises the small amount of liner showing. Alternatively, if the outer skin of the pool is built from brick or blockwork, the liner can be taken part-way through it and sandwiched in the middle of the wall.

The liner for a stream can be laid over a smooth concrete base and covered with wet mortar. It can be completely concealed by stones tipped onto the stream bed when the mortar is still wet. This is where your imagination comes in. Make the feature as natural as possible, using larger stones to create pools and divisions within the stream.

Whether they are formal or informal in design, waterfalls need careful construction to ensure that they are fully watertight. Any leakage of water can eventually lead to the circulating system running dry and damage to the pump.

During the construction of even the most natural watercourse you need to keep a constant check on levels from side to side, gradients and the depth of pools. An excellent tip is to have liners of ample size. If you need to use more than one sheet, overlap the top over the bottom so that the water flows smoothly off one and onto the next.

pre-formed pools

These are the easiest pools to install as they can be bought off the peg in a wide variety of shapes and sizes. The smaller pools are less useful as they cannot maintain the correct balance of plants, fish and other aquatic life. Free-form shapes are far too convoluted for use in an architectural design, but they may fit into the less formal parts of the garden, particularly if the edges are completely concealed by coping or planting.

Pools are usually constructed from black fibreglass, as this is a tough material and relatively light and easy to handle. Marginal shelves for aquatic species planted in baskets are incorporated 25cm (10in) below the water line, but the maximum depth of approximately 45cm (18in) is not deep enough for large fish, such as koi carp, which need far more spacious conditions in which to live.

Opposite above and below *Pre-formed pools are relatively quick and easy to install. The outline of the pool should be marked out and dug down to the level of the marginal shelf. Trace the outline of the deepest area and dig out to the finished depth. Bed the pool on sand or sifted soil, then backfill around the edges, compacting the sand or soil carefully to prevent the pool from moving. Bed the surrounding coping rocks securely in mortar. Natural stone coping like this is ideal around a pre-formed pool as it completely conceals the edges. There is a good balance of pond life here, with lilies and marginal plants offering an excellent environment for fish. Planting outside the pool helps to blend it into the wider setting.*

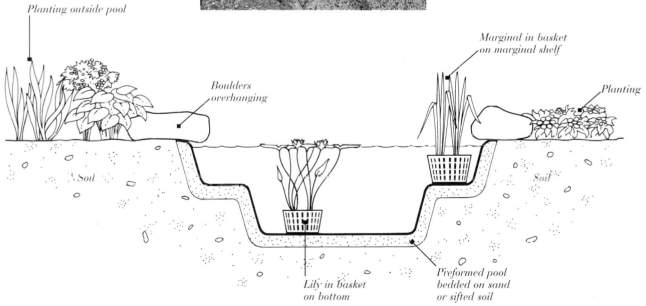

Planting outside pool

Boulders overhanging

Marginal in basket on marginal shelf

Planting

Soil

Soil

Lily in basket on bottom

Preformed pool bedded on sand or sifted soil

concrete

Concrete is time consuming to use and older ponds can begin to leak on account of subsidence or other external influences. Such leaks are often almost impossible to find and as a consequence the feature either becomes redundant or needs complete rebuilding. There are situations, however, where concrete really is the best material to use. The awkward angles and inter-connecting shapes of a number of pools or linked features would be very difficult to construct with a liner, particularly if there is a fall from one level to another.

The real secret to working in concrete is to use suitable reinforcement and to build up the work in layers. Sound and well-compacted foundations are essential and, in an informal situation, wire mesh or chain-link fence is sandwiched in the middle of the work to provide integral strength. With more formal work, timber shuttering is used to contain the concrete, bent steel reinforcing rods tying the bottom and sides together. In order to keep the whole structure waterproof, a suitable additive must be incorporated into the mix. A final coat of a black waterproof paint is generally used to finish the job.

Above right and right *This is a simple concrete block pool with a waterproof, rendered finish. It is gloriously uncomplicated and, being low key, blends perfectly into the overall garden. The bottom of this pool is a single cast-concrete slab. Hollow concrete block walls are built up over reinforcing rods already set in the bottom section and the blocks are then filled with more concrete to stabilize the whole structure completely. A waterproof render is then applied and finished with a black sealant.*

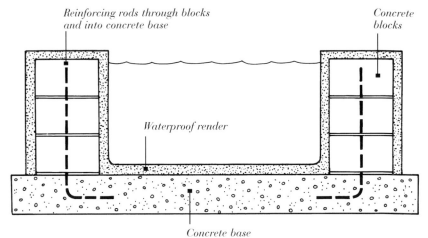

Reinforcing rods through blocks and into concrete base

Concrete blocks

Waterproof render

Concrete base

Right and below *This is an elegant and complex feature of a highly architectural nature. Anyone contemplating building such an arrangement would be well advised to employ a specialist landscape contractor. Water bubbles from the bowl, spilling over into the top pool and the rill, which then descends to the lower rill and pool. The rills and pools are made from concrete that was cast in timber shutters in order to achieve very precise measurements. The whole feature is rendered with waterproof mortar and the surrounding paving laid as a neat coping. Reinforcing rods will be necessary throughout the construction to ensure rigidity and prevent cracking. The diamond pattern of the cobbles complements the paving around the fountain in the foreground.*

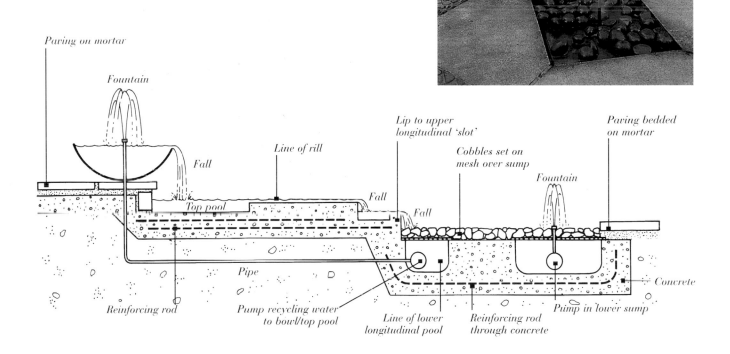

Paving on mortar

Fountain

Line of rill

Lip to upper longitudinal 'slot'

Cobbles set on mesh over sump

Paving bedded on mortar

Fall

Fountain

Fall

Fall

Top pool

Pipe

Concrete

Reinforcing rod

Pump recycling water to bowl/top pool

Line of lower longitudinal pool

Reinforcing rod through concrete

Pump in lower sump

other materials

I have already whetted your appetite for those small-scale water features that can be so neatly tucked into a corner, or become the focus of a small, intimate area. Although most of them use the 'pump and sump' principle, sound construction is essential if they are to work properly. Again, the real secret is to conceal all of the working parts, so that the whole composition looks as natural as possible.

In broad terms, there are two types of feature, those set above ground, in some kind of raised area, or those placed at ground level with the sump buried out of sight. Relatively small features look most attractive set above ground. This brings the whole arrangement closer to eye level and, if set within a raised bed and given generous coping, it can double as an occasional seat. In my experience, a larger sump is always better than a small one. It needs topping up less often and there is more room to work. Plastic or alkathene water tanks are ideal and these can be placed within a raised bed and positioned on a layer of sand or sifted soil.

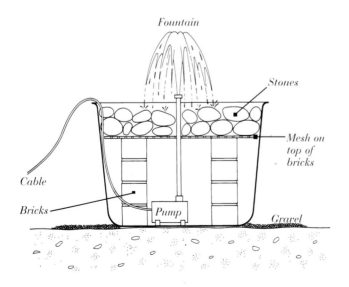

Left and above *This kind of feature is very easy to construct. Ideally, it should be tucked into a corner and surrounded by planting, as it is here, as this helps it to form a natural part of the composition. It is driven by a small, submersible pump set at the bottom of the bowl. Bricks are built up from the bottom to support a wire mesh, which in turn supports cobbles of various sizes. Fill with water, switch the pump on and allow the fountain to dance over the stones. Maintenance includes keeping the surface clear of leaves and debris, as well as topping up during hot weather.*

Left and below *Garden design is an art form. I have a great love of reflective surfaces, particularly when they are associated with water, and I created this hemisphere from stainless steel in a straightforward 'pump and sump' design with the water bubbling gently from top to bottom. The whole arrangement rests in a sea of glass beads that sparkle in the sun. Beneath the feature lies a tank, rather bigger than the hemisphere, inside which are built piers that support both the hemisphere and a fine metal mesh that prevents the beads falling through into the water. Incorporate a removable section of mesh so that you can reach the pump if necessary and then have fun pouring out those sparkling beads.*

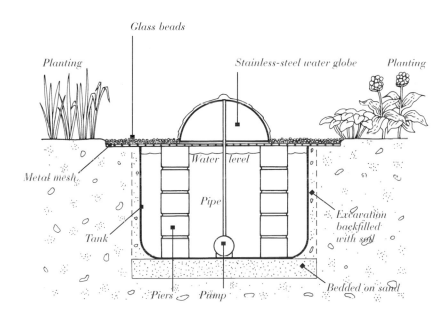

Glass beads

Planting

Stainless-steel water globe

Planting

Metal mesh

Water level

Pipe

Excavation backfilled with soil

Tank

Piers   Pump

Bedded on sand

Make sure the tank is absolutely level and build suitable piers inside it to support your chosen feature. This could be a large, smooth boulder, millstone or anything else your imagination comes up with. The piers should finish just below the top of the tank. A submersible pump at the bottom of the tank provides the power to drive the water contained within the feature. Remember that electricity is lethal and always seek professional help if in the slightest doubt. If the feature is surrounded by loose stones or cobbles you will need to fit some kind of mesh, strong enough to carry the weight involved. Plastic-coated steel can be particularly useful; leave a removable section so that you can reach the pump if necessary. This overall principle of construction can also be used for sunken features. A dipstick is useful for checking the water level.

Smaller features can be constructed within a glazed bowl or timber half-barrel. The workings are exactly the same but a flexible butyl or plastic liner will be needed to keep the barrel watertight. Such arrangements can be delightful when planted with miniature aquatics, a bubble jet just breaking the water's surface.

You will find many kits sold in garden centres that include all the necessary working parts for a complete feature. You can build these in their entirety or buy the components separately, as I have described, to build something unique. Over to you!

Opposite '*Less is more*' – *the battle cry of the Modern Movement – is as pertinent today as it was some 60 years ago. There is an austere and beautiful simplicity about this juxtaposition of natural and man-made elements. The contrast between them emphasizes the qualities of both. The wonderful, deep pink lily stands out against the concrete wall. The fact that the wall is subtly patterned adds background texture to the composition.*

bog gardens

Bog gardens are ideal for plant lovers and there are a huge variety of plants that will thrive in such conditions and provide spectacular displays. However, there is more to the art of making a bog garden than simply creating a wet and stagnant area in the middle of your lawn. The secret is to maintain moisture in the earth rather than creating an area of standing water, which would quite literally suffocate the plants. Bog gardens look best when they adjoin a pool or stream, although they can also be constructed as free-standing features in the garden.

A flexible liner offers the easiest foundation for the garden. If the bog is an extension of a pool or stream, the liner should be bedded over a smooth concrete strip foundation, just below the water level of the adjoining feature. It should then be sandwiched between stones set in mortar. These stones stabilize the bank and allow water to seep into the boggy area.

The liner should be laid over a layer of gravel, which in turn is placed over sand or sifted soil. Punch holes in the liner approximately 60cm (24in) apart and spread a layer of gravel over the top to ensure adequate drainage. The feature should then be topped up with good quality top soil, bringing it slightly proud of the surrounding surface to allow for settlement. The soil should be approximately 30cm (12in) deep.

The method of construction is similar for a free-standing bog garden, but this will obviously need to be kept damp with either an irrigation system or by hand watering.

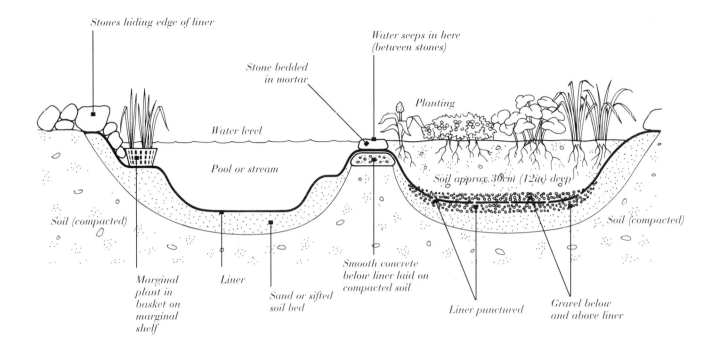

Stones hiding edge of liner

Stone bedded
in mortar

Water seeps in here
(between stones)

Planting

Water level

Pool or stream

Soil approx. 30cm (12in) deep

Soil (compacted)

Soil (compacted)

Marginal
plant in
basket on
marginal
shelf

Liner

Sand or sifted
soil bed

Smooth concrete
below liner laid on
compacted soil

Liner punctured

Gravel below
and above liner

Opposite and above *Rich, rich planting is the stuff of bog gardens, full of flowers and foliage that thrive in such damp conditions. This stream margin gently rises above water level, boasting a wide range of different-coloured iris and bog primulas. The success of this scheme lies in the bold use of drifts, rather than individual specimens. The liner that forms the open water will have to be extended. This is done in such a way that water can just seep between stones set in mortar. You should incorporate a concrete strip foundation beneath the liner as this will prevent erosion. In the bog garden area, gravel should be laid both below and above the liner to aid drainage.*

pumps & equipment

The area that has improved above all others in water garden construction is that of pumps and associated fittings. Submersible pumps now come in a huge range of sizes and specifications. Go to a good aquatic centre and find the right pump for the job. As with most other things in this field, concealment is the name of the game and a pump should be positioned beneath an overhang of rock or in the shadow of a stepping stone. Pipework to transport water to the top of the feature should also be carefully concealed. The pipes are normally buried, which is quite satisfactory until you forget where they are and puncture them with a garden fork! Accidents can be avoided by marking the position of the pipe with stones so that you always remember where it is.

It is almost inevitable that you will want to adjust the flow to a fountain, waterfall or other arrangement and in this case it should be simple enough to fit a gate valve, usually right next to the pump, in an easily accessible position. Larger above-ground pumps are sometimes used for major projects. These are more problematic, however, requiring complicated pipework, and need to be housed in chambers which are often unsightly. If you are contemplating such a major project, then this is almost certainly best left to a specialist contractor.

Right and opposite *Although it looks impressive, this kind of feature is easy enough to construct, working on the 'pump and sump' principle. The trellis sits on the edge of the copper container, a pipe being neatly disguised by one of the slats. This is connected to the top cup and water spills from one to the next, eventually falling back into the sump. It is essential that the pump is fitted with a valve so the flow can be delicately adjusted and does not simply gush all over the feature.*

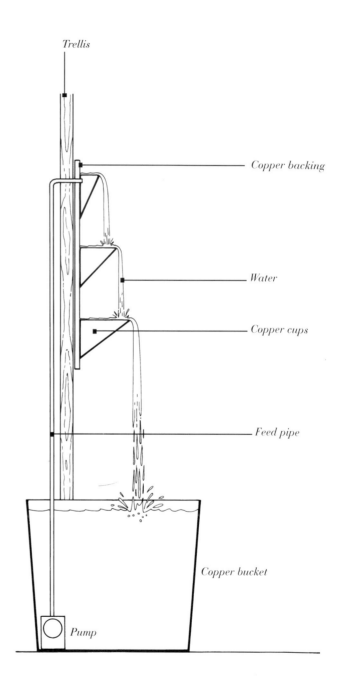

Trellis

Copper backing

Water

Copper cups

Feed pipe

Copper bucket

Pump

electricity

Electricity is the driving force for most water features. It is absolutely essential to use it sensibly and install it correctly. If in doubt enlist the services of a qualified electrician, as it is far better to be safe than sorry. Power to pumps can be mains voltage for the larger types, or stepped down – often to 12 volts – via a transformer. All equipment bought from a reputable garden centre will include full installation instructions that should be followed to the letter. If running a number of features, pumps or lights it can make sense to install a ring main around the garden. This will provide specially waterproofed power points that make connections far easier. Installing a ring main is usually a professional job. Cables should be armoured and buried at a safe depth so that they cannot be reached by garden tools.

If you are carrying out a complete redesign of the garden, or starting from scratch, it can make good sense to plan the cable runs right at the beginning when it will be easy to dig any necessary trenches and lay the cables. The planned features can always be built and connected at a later date. Never underestimate the number of places that you may need power and aim to be slightly over, rather than under, capacity.

lighting

When you think about it, our gardens and the features contained within them are dark for approximately half the year. While we primarily use the space during daylight, there is enormous scope for evening and night-time use, which is where lighting comes into its own. Subtlety is everything with garden lighting, 'less is more' being a sensible principle. Even simple lights can cast a complexity of shadows.

Water features are always focal points, whatever their size, and it follows that lighting should focus on them, leaving the immediate surroundings to act as a quiet backdrop. Before you think about anything else, consider colour for a moment. Forget all the garish hues like yellow, red and orange, as they turn foliage revolting colours. Blue and white light are by far the best to use, enhancing the surroundings rather than detracting from them.

Different lighting techniques produce different effects and the simplest are floodlighting and spotlighting. Spotlights use a hidden source and a tight beam to pinpoint a feature and throw it into sharp relief, while floodlights provide a softer and rather gentler spread of light. Backlighting is just what it says: a relatively low light source behind the feature, again throwing it into relief in an altogether more subtle way.

Stunning effects can be obtained by using waterproof lighting set within a pool or stream, making the feature literally glow from within. If you want the ultimate special effect, then experiment with the wonderful world of fibre optics that can hang like glowing mare's tails down a watercourse.

Right *When lighting is combined sensitively with water the results can be magical. Here the white light source is placed below the water level, picking out the edge of the stepping stone in sharp relief, and contrasting with the darker foreground paving. There is just enough ambient illumination to light the blooms that seem to float against the near-black background.*

care & maintenance

Maintenance should be preventative and not just curative. Checking features and their surrounds regularly and doing small repairs where necessary is more sensible than performing major reconstruction work after something has gone drastically wrong. In my own garden maintenance has become part of an almost unconscious daily or weekly routine. I regularly check watercourses for leaks, clean pump filters and make sure any cables, sockets and other electrical equipment are in good condition. The brickwork or stonework of raised pools or other features may need repointing from time to time and it will be particularly important to check the coping around pools. Unsound coping could result in a nasty accident or even the drowning of an unsuspecting child.

It is a good idea to install a leaf net in autumn, particularly if there are nearby trees. This can be left in place for a month or so and then removed, the contents being ideal for the compost heap. If leaves are not removed from the water's surface, or prevented from settling there in the first place, they can lead to

Above right Reflections are the crowning glory of still or gently rippled water, but to achieve this degree of clarity there needs to be a perfect ecological balance, or a sophisticated filtration system. The former is preferable.

Right Leaves in this situation form a richly patterned aquatic carpet which is frankly gorgeous. However, you should be aware that a substantial build-up of leaves can lead to the release of methane gas. This may be dangerous for fish if the pond freezes over. A leaf net could be the answer.

Opposite A beautifully planted pool. Remember, however, that many of these plants are rampant and need thinning on an annual basis, to the benefit of your friends of course!

blockages in the pump which can in turn lead to costly repairs. In my pools I have two relatively large pumps and both have performed perfectly for six years. Sooner or later one will fail and so I have a brand new one in

Rich planting turns a man-made pool into a feature that blends into the surroundings and looks natural. A pool this size is big enough to create its own ecosystem that will take care of a lot of the maintenance on it own, but a helping hand will be needed once in a while. Most of the plants here will need thinning out at least once a year in order to prevent the pool becoming completely swamped with planting.

reserve which can quickly be installed to minimize disruption. In summer, waterfalls can provide fish with invaluable oxygen so it can be dangerous to leave them out of action for any length of time.

Occasionally pool liners can get holed or split – one very good reason for encasing them in concrete. Should an exposed liner be punctured by a fork or a misdirected arrow it can be patched. Remember to leave the offending object in place so that you can find the hole easily. The closer this is to the surface the easier the job will be, as the pool or watercourse will need draining down to that point and then cleaning off and drying. Patch kits can be bought from a water garden specialist and a square of new liner stuck over the hole and allowed to dry completely before refilling.

Maintenance should be preventative

and not just curative

Right *There are moments of creation that need no description. Look, feel and understand.*

planting

Plants will bring your water feature to life, softening the edges of a pool or rill, introducing colour and interest throughout the year and blending everything into the wider garden landscape. Planting in water is easy as long as you understand a few basic techniques – and believe me, the effort is more than worthwhile.

planting

Any area of water needs to have a balanced ecosystem encompassing plants, fish and a whole range of insects and other life forms. Together, these will ensure a healthy environment, but without them, even with expensive and complicated pumps, filters and incidental equipment, it will be almost impossible to prevent algae and other problems. The balance of a pond depends on a number of things, the most simple of which are sunlight, mineral salts, oxygen and carbon dioxide. A pool without plants allows algae to use the sun's energy, together with the salts, which in turn makes the water green. Algae can grow incredibly quickly. They will choke your pool and prevent you from being able to see the fish and other inhabitants.

A well-stocked pond uses submerged species that feed on the salts, marginal plants that grow with their toes in the water and other plants, such as lilies, that have floating leaves. By shading approximately half the pond's surface the lily pads reduce the available sunlight and the energy that it provides for algae.

Right *Planting in a pool can be as simple or as complicated as you want it to be. It would be difficult to improve on the classical beauty of lilies.*
Opposite *A richer ecological habitat is achieved with a richer mix of planting, including ferns and arum lilies.*

Above *There is always a wonderful visual dialogue between horizontal water and vertical foliage. Horizontal foliage floats on the surface of the water, such as these great lily pads with their shining flowers, whereas vertical foliage stands upright from, or falls down into, the pool with the movement of the water.*

Most plants for water features can be obtained from good water garden centres along with any equipment you may require. All plants, apart from a few that actually float on the surface of the water, need to be planted. You can buy perforated planting baskets to do this, but it is an excellent idea to think ahead, if possible, and to build in planting beds while you are actually constructing the pond. These beds can be incorporated around the edge of the pool area, just below the water line for marginal plants, and in deep water for the plants with floating leaves. If you are using a liner, you can build the beds on top of it, but remember that you will need a simple foundation underneath to carry the weight.

Plants provide stability for both the banks and the eye, creating points of interest along the way

Aquatic plants should be grown in good quality top soil which can be used to fill both built-in beds and movable planting baskets. You should line the baskets with hessian to prevent the soil from washing out of them, and top the soil with a layer of gravel for the same reason. My own pools are pretty big and I have used large plastic crates as planters for lilies and cut down plastic dustbins for my marginals, both of which allow ample room for development. Plants are not particularly fussy about what type of container they grow in, but make sure it is black as this makes it less visible.

Although you can plant during most of the summer, late spring is best, when growth is vigorous and the water is starting to warm up. Aquatics need very little attention beyond thinning out. This can be quite drastic for very vigorous species. I have a big sort-out in spring. This involves cutting back and

Above *Streams are full of movement, swirling and ever changing. Plants provide stability for both the banks and the eye, creating points of interest along the way. These mimulus will thrive in such conditions.*

removing plants from their containers to divide them. It can be hard work and two people make it much easier to shift the big containers. In a thriving water system like mine, you need a second, slightly less drastic, session in late summer, which thins things out again and opens up all the right sight lines.

We have already discussed bog gardens, with their ideal growing conditions for all those wonderful damp-loving, large-leafed species, as well as the delightful primulas, marsh marigolds and iris. Very often, however, your pool will be set in the midst of a garden which has far drier conditions. There are many plants that will grow in both wet or dry areas, including iris, bamboo, grasses, hostas, lythrum, lysimachia and dierama. With a little irrigation you can extend the range considerably. If you have room, think about incorporating the wonderful and giant *Gunnera manicata* and the slightly less rampant *Rheum palmatum*.

As far as maintenance is concerned, there should be very little if everything is balanced out correctly. There is a lot of nonsense talked about draining pools and cleaning them out, which invariably destroys the eco-system and most of the insect life. Obviously, if an old pool is completely silted up it does need attention, but my pools are now six years old and are nowhere near a clear-out. In other words, let sleeping dogs, or pools, lie.

There is always a wonderful visual dialogue between horizontal water and vertical foliage. Horizontal foliage floats on the surface of the water, whereas vertical foliage stands upright from, or falls down into, the pool with the movement of the water.

Above *Astilbes are one of the best waterside or bog garden plants and once the blooms have finished I leave the brown seed heads on throughout the winter as they look so attractive. Flower colour includes red, pink and white.*

fish

& wildlife

I'm something of a child when it comes to ponds. I love to watch the creatures that live in the water. There are fish darting about, dragonflies hatching and bees coming to drink. The wonderful thing is that most of this just happens without our interference. Get the basics right and the rest follows naturally.

fish & wildlife

Plants combine with fish, insects and all kinds of other creatures, to build up a complete and low-maintenance ecosystem. This in turn provides a wonderful attraction for birds, toads and frogs which will live off the aquatic environment you have created. You can be serious or laid back about all this and I have to admit that I fall into the latter category. Equally, I have to say that it all works a treat.

The secret is to have lots of space, and I do have plenty of water, both still and moving. A purpose-built stream links upper and lower pools and this, now that the planting has developed, works as a natural filter, keeping the whole system crystal clear. My fish have come as fairground prizes and from the original half dozen or so we now have more than I can count, and big

ones too. They are all common goldfish but they have interbred, producing all kinds of colours and fin formations. The pools have ample planting and corners that are secluded enough to encourage breeding. The environment is so rich that I never have to feed the fish. Damsel flies and dragonflies abound with their magical colours, water beetles and water boatmen skate and slide, while frogs hop out at you at the most unexpected moments. I have beaches in the stream that allow the frogs to get out and encourage small mammals to drink. Water snails are there in abundance and must have come in with the plants; they are invaluable as filters.

All I did was to introduce plants and fish; the rest just came along, as they will for you too. Many people complain about mosquitoes around water, and it's true,

Left Attracting visitors such as toads to a water feature plays a vital role in creating and maintaining a healthy and balanced ecosystem.
Opposite A pool in the prime of life with fish, plants and all kinds of other wildlife thriving in abundance. Just watch out for a heron and if necessary stretch a single strand of wire 15cm (6in) above the ground right around the pool as a deterrent.

we do have a few, but more end up as part of a wonderful diet for swallows and frogs than they do feeding on us!

If you are a fish fancier, koi carp may be your speciality. These fish can live quite happily in a natural pool, but some people want perfectly clear water without too much vegetation to get in the way of their expensive pets. In this case you need to fit filtration systems. Although effective, these do seem to produce a clinical end result. It can be useful to have a number of bottom feeders, such as tench, which also help to keep the pool clean.

It is very important to remember to keep an area of water clear in freezing conditions, preventing a build-up of lethal gasses. Never break the ice, as the shock waves can stun fish. You can buy small floating immersion heaters, which are both economic to run and do the job perfectly.

Above left *This kind of habitat is superb around a pool with damp conditions, ample leaf litter and shallow beaches. Don't be over-zealous with maintenance as you could so easily upset this balance!*

Left *Apart from the visual beauty of these stems, they will provide the perfect hatching place for dragonfly larvae. Watch the newly emerged fly dry his wings and depart in all his glory.*

Right *What a fine fellow – and one of your most trusted garden friends who will eat vast quantities of unwelcome guests. Live in harmony with your pond life and they will pay you back a thousandfold.*

address book

Hozelock Cyprio
Haddenham
Aylesbury HP17 8JD
Tel: 01844 291881
Fax: 01844 290344

Liners, equipment, features. Mail order

Intercel House
Main Street
Overseal, Swadlincote
Derbyshire DE12 6LG
Tel/fax: 01283 763666

Equipment. Mail order

Lotus Water Garden Products
Junction Street
Burnley BB12 0NA
Tel: 01282 420771
Fax: 01282 412719

Liners, features. Mail order

Oase
3 Telford Gate
West Portway Industrial Estate
Andover SP10 3SF
Tel: 01264 333225
Fax: 01264 333226

Liners, equipment

Oasis Water Garden Products
Oasis House
Deer Park Industrial Estate
Knowle Lane, Fair Oak
Eastleigh SO50 7PZ
Tel: 01703 602602
Fax: 01703 602603
Web site: www.oasis-water-garden.co.uk

Liners, equipment, features

David Stevens
Corner Cottage
Thornton
Buckinghamshire MK17 0HE
Tel/Fax: 01280 821097
e-mail: gardens@david-stevens.co.uk

International garden design, garden design correspondence course

Society of Garden Designers
The Institute of Horticulture
14/15 Belgrave Square
London SW1X 8PS
Tel: 020 7 838 9311
Fax: 020 7 838 9322

Royal Horticultural Society
80 Vincent Square
London SW1P 2PE
Tel: 020 7 834 4333
Fax: 020 7 828 2304

Association of Professional Landscapers
Creighton Lodge
Hollington Lane
Stramshall, Uttoxeter
Tel: 01889 507256
Fax: 01889 507391
E-mail hta@martex.co.uk

British Association of Landscape Industries (BALI)
Landscape House
9 Henry House
Keighley
W Yorkshire BD21 3DR

British Koi Keepers Society
Information on your nearest section on internet
www.bkks.co.uk

Japanese Garden Society
Groves Mill
Shakers Lane
Long Itchington
Rugby
Tel: 01926 632746

Equipment, Liners, Pre-Formed Pools, Pumps Etc

Aquatics Direct
Silk Street
Congleton
Cheshire
CW12 4BR
Tel: 01260 275144
Fax: 01260 298141

Plants, liners, equipment, features, sundries. Mail order

Bradshaws Direct
Nicholson Link
Clifton Moor
York YO1 1SS
Tel: 01904 691169
Fax; 01904 691133

Bio-Claire International
48 Bathurst Walk
Richings Park
Iver
Bucks SI0 9BH
Tel: 01753 774777
Fax: 01753 774778

Livestock, liners, equipment, features, hard landscaping, sundries

Heissner UK
Regency Business Centre
Queens Road
Kenilworth CV8 1QJ
Tel: 01926 851166
Fax: 01926 851151

Liners, equipment, features

Shirley Aquatics
1355 Stratford Road
Shirley
Solihull B90 4EF
Tel: 0121 744 1300
Fax: 0121 744 0067
Internet: www.shirleyaquatics.co.uk

Plants, livestock, liners,
equipment, features, sundries,
hard landscaping. Mail order

Trident Water Garden
Products
Carlton Road
Foleshill
Coventry CV6 7FL
Tel: 01203 638802
Fax: 01203 637891

Plants, livestock, liners,
equipment, features. Mail order

Paved Areas

Blanc de Bierges
Eastrea Road
Whittlesey
Peterborough PE7 2AG
Tel: 01733 202566
Fax: 01733 205405
E-mail: mail@blancdebierges.com

Modular precast paving

Camas Building Materials
Hulland Ward
Ashbourne
Derbyshire DE6 3ET

Wide range of precast paving

Marshalls Mono Ltd
Southowram
Halifax HX3 9SY
Tel: 01422 306355
Fax: 01422 306190
E-mail:
customer.services@marshalls.co.uk
Web site: www.marshalls.co.uk

Wide range of precast paving

Natural Stone Paving and Rock

Civil Engineering
Developments (CED)
728 London Road
West Thurrock
Grays RM20 3LU
Tel: 01708 867237
Fax: 01708 867230

Literock Ltd
Sherington Nurseries
Sherington
Newport Pagnell MK16 9NQ
Tel: 01908 610236
Fax: 01908 210671

Decking

Leisuredeck Ltd
311 Marsh Road
Leagrave
Luton LU3 2RZ
Tel: 01582 563080
Fax: 01582 563080

Features/Sculpture

Stowasis
Eastgate House
Longborough
Moreton-in-Marsh
Gloucestershire GL56 0QJ
Tel: 01451 83 2525

Fairweather Sculpture
Hillside House, Starston
Norfolk IP20 9NN
Tel: 01379 852266
Fax: 01379 852266

Waterstone Fountains
Tel/Fax: 01934 820967

Simon Percival
Sunnymead Works
Toadsmoor Road
Brimscombe
Gloucestershire GL5 2UF
Tel/Fax: 01453 731478
E-mail: simon-
percival@sculpt.netkonect.co.uk

Wonderful modern designs

Iris Water & Design
Langburn Bank
Castleton
Whitby YO21 2EU
Tel: 01287 660002
Fax: 01287 660004
Internet: www.iriswater.co.uk

Plants & Aquatic Nurseries

Wildwoods Water gardens
Theobalds Park Road
Crews Hill
Enfield EN2 9BP
Tel: 020 8 366 0243
Fax:020 8 366 9892
E-mail: info@woldwoods.co.uk

Stapeley Water Gardens
London Road
Stapeley
Nantwich
Cheshire CW5 7LH
Tel:01270 623868
Fax: 01270 624919
E-mail:
StapeleyWG@btinternet.com

Rowden Gardens
Brentor
Tavistock
Devon Pl19 0NG
Tel: 01822 810275

Kenchester Water Gardens
Church Road
Lyde
Hereford HR1 3AB
Tel: 01432 264222
Fax: 01432 342243

Koi Carp Specialists

Klassik Koi
Clarefarm Garden Centre
Nel Pan lane
Leigh WN7 5LA
Tel/fax: 01942 260000

Nishikoi
Nishikoi Information Centre
PO Box 5584
Braintree CM7 4EX
E-mail: infocentre@nishikoi.com

Tropikoi Aquatics
Lynn Road
Wisbech
Cambridgeshire PE14 7DA
Tel: 01945 585458

Tewin Mill Koi Centre
Tewin Mill
Kingsbridge
Tewin
Welwyn AL6 0LJ
Tel: 01438 716019
Fax; 01438 840096

index

Page numbers in *italics* refer
to illustrations.

A
algae 80
aquatic centres 56, 70, 83
aquatic planting 14, 66, 83–4
architectural effects 12, *37*,
     55, 63
astilbes 52, *53*, *85*
asymmetric style 24, *24–5*

B
baskets 42, *61*, *69*, 83
beaches *36*, 88
     construction *58*
birds 28, 88, 90
bog gardens 28, 33, 52, *52–3*,
     68, *68–9*, 84
boulders 12, *26*, *27*, 28, *47*,
     48, 66
bowls 16, *30*, *40*, 42, 48, 66
budgeting 14

C
canals 34–7, *34–7*
care 30, 44, 74–6
children 28, 48, 74

choosing a style 20–7
classical water features 42,
     44, *44*
cobbles *20*, *25*, 28, *31*, *36*, 46,
     48, *63*
concrete 8, 62, *67*, 76, 68
construction 14, 54, 55
     beaches *58*
     fountains *63*, *64*, 65
     pools *56*, *58*, *61*, *62*, *69*
     waterfalls *59*, *70*
coping 33, *57*, 60, *63*, 74
copper features 43, 44, *70–1*
costs 14

D
Dadaism *21*
decking *19*, *24*, *25*, 26, 33

E
ecosystem 30, 60, 80, 84, 88
electricity 66, 72, 74
equipment 12, 70, 80

F
fashion 8, 20
filters 74, 80, 88, 90

fish 6, 28, 30, 38, 60, 76, 80,
     87, 88–90, *91*
flow adjustment 48, 70
focal points 16, 33, 38, *48*
foliage 39, *50*, 52, 72, *82*
formal style 8, 12, *19*, 22,
     22–3, *31*, 34, *34*
fountains 34, 38–40, *38–41*,
     70
     bubble fountains *33*,
          38, 66
     construction *63*, *64*, 65
frogs 88, 90, *91*

G
garden buildings 24, 33
garden centres 12, 42, 56, 66,
     83
garden design 11, 12, 20, 44
garden rooms 22, *37*, 44
glass beads 48, *65*
Gunnera manicata 52, *52*, 84

H
habitat 6, 28, 30, 60, 80, 84,
     88
hedges *20*, *22*, *33*
historical influences 6, *14*,
     34, 40

horizontals *8*, *26*, 34, 82
hostas *46*, 52, 84
house/garden link 6–8, *17*,
     18, *19*, 20, 24, 30, 34
humour 16, *28*

I
informal style 12, 26, *26–7*
insects 30, 80, 84, 87, 88
inspiration 12, 28
iris 52, *53*, 84

K
kugels 8, 40

L
leaf nets 74–6
leaks 60, 62, 74, 76
lighting 50, 72, *73*
lilies 34, *64*?, 80, *80*, *81*, *82*
liners *56–9*, 56–60, 66, 68, 76
     repairing 76
Lutyens, Sir Edwin 34
lythrum *53*, 84

M
maintenance 30, 44, 74–6
masks 16, 42–4

Mediterranean garden *51*
mesh *64, 65*, 66
millstones 8, 46, 66
Modern Movement 24, *67*
moodboards 12
mosquitoes 30, 88–90
movement 6, *9, 20, 36*, 37, 50, *83*

N
natural effects 26, *37*, 55
    studying natural features 12, 37

O
oxygenation 14, 38, 76, 80

P
paths 22
paving 14, *19*, 24, *33, 35, 63*
Perspex *38*, 44, 50
piers *65*, 66
pipes 44, 46, 48, 70
planting *26*, 28, 42, 50
    aquatic 14, 66, 83–4
    planting beds 83
plants 6, 12, 28, 30, 78, *32*, 34, 52, *53*, 60, 80, *81*, 84
pools 11, 12, 16, 28, *30–3*, 30–3, 56, 68, 78
    construction 56, *58, 61, 62, 69*
    draining 76, 84
    pre-formed pools 60, *61*
primulas 52, *53*, 84

pumps 14, 38, 44, 46–8, 64–6, 70, *70–1*, 74–6, 80
pyramids *37, 40*

R
reflections 6, *15*, 16, *20, 21*, 33, *33*, 40, 50, *65*, 74
Rheum palmatum 52, 84
rills 12, *19*, 22, 28, *31*, 34–7, *34–7*, 56, 78
rock 12, 14, *26, 27*, 37, *37*

S
safety 28, 48, 72, 74
slides 12, *29*, 48
small-scale features *14*, 16, *30*, 42, 46–8, 46–9, 64–6, *64–6*, 70–1
sound 6, 16, 38, 44, 50
spheres 8, 40
spouts 16, *42*
stainless steel 40, 48, *65*
streams 34–7, *34–7*, 56, 60, 68, 88
structural features 50, *50–1*
styles 20–7
sumps 44, 46–8, 64–6

T
tanks *64, 65*, 64–6
taps *45*
terraces 14, 22, 24, 33
thinning out 83–4
toads 88, *88*
trees 12, 14, *18, 23*, 24, 74

V
verticals *8, 18, 26*, 34, *37*, 82
views 16, *19*, 22, 33

W
walls 14
    wall-mounted features 42–4, *42–5*
water curtains *51*
water ports 28, *29*, 50
water stairs 22, 50
waterfalls *27*, 56, 60, 70, 76
    construction *59, 70*
wildlife *6*, 14, 28, 88–90

First published in 2000 by Conran Octopus Limited
a part of Octopus Publishing Group
2-4 Heron Quays London E14 4JP

www.conran-octopus.co.uk

Text copyright © David Stevens 2000
Design and layout copyright © Conran Octopus 2000

Commissioning Editor: Stuart Cooper
Senior Editor: Helen Woodhall
Copy Editor: Helena Attlee
Editorial Assistant: Alexandra Kent

Creative Director: Leslie Harrington
Designer: Lucy Gowans
Picture Researcher: Mel Watson
Production: Zoe Fawcett

British Library Cataloguing-in-Publication Data
A catalogue record for this book is available from the British Library

ISBN 1 84091 115 8

Colour origination by Sang Choy International, Singapore
Printed in China

Author's acknowledgments

A finished book is only the tip of an iceberg of planning and hard work involving far more people than the author! Special thanks to my editor, Helen Woodhall and my secretary, Angela Bambridge.

Publisher's acknowledgments

The publisher would like to thank the following photographers and agencies for their kind permission to reproduce the photographs in this book:
2 Jerry Harpur/Designer: Jean-Pierre Delettre, Chaumont-sur-Loire, France,1998; 4–5 Tamarra Richards/The Garden Picture Library; 7 Deborah Davis/Photonica; 8 left Lanny Provo; 8 right Bart van Leuven/Landscape Architects: Wilfried Buls & Paul Claes, Belgium; 9 K.Hashimoto/Photonica; 10–11 Andrew Lawson/Hampton Court Flower Show 1999/Designer: Karen Maskell; 13 Christi Carter/ The Garden Picture Library/ Designer: Kent Gullickson, Ca, USA; 14 above Steven Wooster/ Designer: Anthony Paul; 14 below Clive Nichols/Chelsea Flower Show 1997/Designer:Roger Platts; 15 Simon Kenny/Belle Magazine/Architect: Mike Macaulay, Australia; 16 Liz Eddison; 17 Gil Hanly/ Owner: Dr. M Pohl, Auckland, New Zealand; 18 Earl Carter/Belle Magazine/ Metropolis Urban Space Design, Melbourne, Australia; 18 below Bart van Leuven/ Landscape Architect:Claes en Humblet Tuinarchitecten NV, Belgium; 19 below Ian Pleeth/Acres Wild Garden Design; 20 John Glover/ Hampton Court Flower Show 1995/ Designer:Naila Green; 21 Leigh Clapp/Living Exteriors Garden Design, Australia; 22 left Liz Eddison/Chelsea Flower Show 1999/Christie's Fine Art Auctioneers/ Designer: George Carter; 22 right Jerry Harpur/Hazleby House, Berkshire; 23 Leigh Clapp/ Designer: Swinburne TAFE, Australia; 24 left Marijke Heuff/Mien Ruys, Holland; 24 above right Malcolm Birkett/Designer: John Brookes/Kings Heath Park, Birmingham; 24 below right Bart van Leuven/ Landscape Architect: Jean Noel Capart; 25 N et P Mioulane/Mise au Point/Designer: Christophe Caixtois; 26 left Gary Rogers/ The Garden Picture Library; 26 above right Ian Smith/ Acres Wild Garden Design; 26 below right Gil Hanly/ Garden Design by Isabelle Greene and Associates, FASLA, Santa Barbara Landscape Architect; 27 Roger Foley/Designers: Oehme, van Sweden & Associates; 28 Marijke Heuff/Artist: Tamas Asszonyi; 29 Marianne Majerus/Hampton Court Flower Show 1999 /Designer:David Stevens; 30 John Glover; 31 Brigitte Thomas/The Garden Picture Library/ Designer: J. Wirtz, Belgium; 32 Brigitte Perdereau/ Plantbessin Garden, France; 33 Ian Smith/ Acres Wild Garden Design; 34 Gary Rogers; 35 Undine Prohl; 36 John Glover/Hampton Court Flower Show 1992; 37 left Roger Foley/ Designer: Sam Williamson and Associates, USA; 37 right Marianne Majerus/Designer: Marc Schollen; 38 John Glover/Hampton Court Flower Show 1994/ Horticultural Therapy; 39 Elizabeth Whiting & Associates; 40 left John Glover/National Rose Society Garden/ Sculptor: William Pye; 40 right Jerry Harpur/ Designer: Brent Collins & Associates, Hong Kong; 41 John Glover/Chelsea Flower Show 1995/Designer Fiona Lawrenson; 42 Andrew Lawson; 43 Justyn Willsmore/Hampton Court Flower Show 1997/Chenies Aquatics; 44 J S Sira/ The Garden Picture Library/Chelsea Flower Show 1994/ Haddonstone Ltd; 45 Bart van Leuven/ Landscape Architects: Wilfried Buls & Paul Claes, Belgium; 46 John Glover/Designer: Alan Titchmarsh; 47 Gary Rogers; 48 Mark Bolton; 49 Leigh Clapp/ Mistilis Garden, Australia; 50 Malcolm Birkett/Chelsea Flower Show 1999/ Marie Curie Cancer Care Garden/Designer: Patrick McCann; 51 Andrew Lawson/ Chelsea Flower Show 1998/ Designer: David Stevens; 52 Marianne Majerus, Bushy Park; 53 above Andrew Lawson/Marwood Hill, Devon; 53 below Marianne Majerus/ Fairhaven Garden Trust, Norfolk; 54–55 John Glover; 57 Brigitte Thomas/ The Garden Picture Library; 58 Liz Eddison; 59 Liz Eddison/ Designers: Bunny Guinness and Peter Eustance, Chelsea Flower Show 1999, Wyevale Garden Centres; 61 John Glover; 62 Michael Paul/ The Garden Picture Library/Designer: Anthony Paul; 63 Andrew Lawson/Designer: Paul Bangay, Australia; 64 Clive Nichols; 65 Andrew Lawson/ Hampton Court Flower Show 1999/ Designer: David Stevens; 67 Lanny Provo; 68 Andrew Lawson/ Marwood Hill, Devon; 71 Derek St Romaine/ Hampton Court Flower Show 1994/Age Concern/ Designer: Barbara Hunt; 73 Marianne Majerus; 74 above Trevor Mein/Belle Magazine/ Landscape Design: Andrew McFarland, Australia; 74 below S & O Mathews; 75 Ron Sutherland/ The Garden Picture Library/Eco Design, Australia; 76 Brigitte Perdereau/ Chaumont-sur-Loire, France; 77 Andrew Lawson/ Designer: Tom Sitta, Australia; 78–79 Roger Foley; 80 Ursel Borstell; 81 Ron Sutherland/ The Garden Picture Library/ Designer: Anthony Paul; 82 Roger Foley/Designers: Oehme, van Sweden & Associates; 83 Sunniva Harte/ The Garden Picture Library; 85 S & O Mathews/ Cobblers, Sussex; 86–87 Justyn Willsmore/ RHS Wisley, Surrey; 88 David Bevan; 89 Justyn Willsmore/ RHS Wisley, Surrey; 90 above Angela Hampton/ Ecoscene; 90 below J C Mayer – G Le Scanff/The Garden Picture Library/Jardin de Talos, France; 91 Paul Stevens/Planet Earth Pictures.

We apologize in advance for any unintentional omission and would be pleased to insert the appropriate acknowledgment in any subsequent edition.